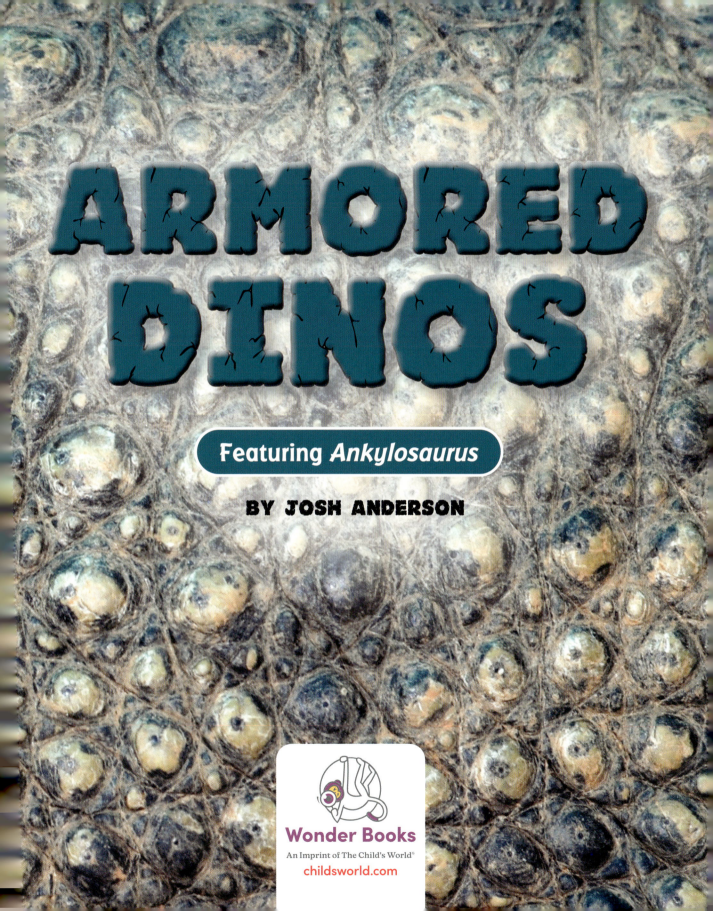

ARMORED DINOS

Featuring *Ankylosaurus*

BY JOSH ANDERSON

Wonder Books
An Imprint of The Child's World®
childsworld.com

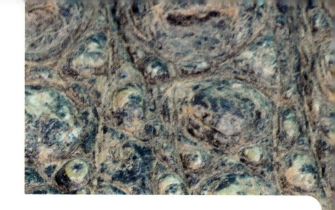

Published by The Child's World®
800-599-READ • www.childsworld.com

Copyright © 2023 by The Child's World®
All rights reserved. No part of this book may be reproduced or utilized in any form or by any means without written permission from the publisher.

Photography Credits
Cover: ©Suwat wongkham / Shutterstock; page 1: ©Pan Xunbin / Shutterstock; page 5: ©DE AGOSTINI PICTURE LIBRARY / Contributor / Getty Images; page 6: ©Roberto Machado Noa / Contributor / Getty Images; page 9: ©DE AGOSTINI PICTURE LIBRARY / Contributor / Getty Images; page 10: ©Roberto Machado Noa / Contributor / Getty Images; page 11: ©Zhenyakot / Shutterstock; page 13: ©DE AGOSTINI PICTURE LIBRARY / Contributor / Getty Images; page 14: ©DE AGOSTINI PICTURE LIBRARY / Contributor / Getty Images; page 16: ©Tuul & Bruno Morandi / Getty Images; page 16: ©Julio Francisco; page 17: ©Julio Francisco; page 19: ©Roberto Machado Noa / Contributor / Getty Images; page 21: ©Alexandre Morin-Laprise / Getty Images

ISBN Information
9781503865211 (Reinforced Library Binding)
9781503865839 (Portable Document Format)
9781503866676 (Online Multi-user eBook)
9781503867512 (Electronic Publication)

LCCN 2022940909

Printed in the United States of America

About the Author

Josh Anderson has published more than 50 books for children and young adults. His two sons, Leo and Dane, are the greatest joys in his life. Josh's hobbies include coaching youth basketball, no-holds-barred games of Exploding Kittens, reading, and family movie nights. His favorite dinosaur is a secret he'll never share!

CONTENTS

Digging for Bones…4

What We Know…11

Keep Searching…18

Glossary…22
Wonder More…23
Learn More…24
Index…24

CHAPTER 1

Digging for Bones

Pretend you can time travel to a prehistoric age . . . . You've gone back about 66 million years. It's the very end of the dinosaur age. The K–T extinction event will occur soon. You spot a creature eating a fern plant. It pulls the leaves off with its narrow beak. The creature's body is covered in bony plates. The plates are similar to those on a crocodile or armadillo. You realize this must be an armored dinosaur. You're looking at an *Ankylosaurus* (ang-kuh-loh-SAWR-uss).

You spot a *Tyrannosaurus rex* (teh-rahn-uh-SAWR-uss REKS) in the distance. So does the *Ankylosaurus*. But it just keeps on eating. A full-grown *Ankylosaurus* would've probably been safe from most meat-eaters. Its wide, bony body protected it from attacks.

How do we know so much about creatures who lived millions of years before the first humans? The simple answer: SCIENCE! Let's learn more!

Ankylosaurus has been used in many video games and animated shows about dinosaurs.

The osteoderms on an *Ankylosaurus* are also known as "scutes."

Humans have been studying *Ankylosaurus* for more than 110 years. The first discovery of a partial *Ankylosaurus* fossil was in 1906. The bones were discovered in Montana. A team from the American Museum of Natural History found the bones. The museum described *Ankylosaurus* as a "remarkably interesting dinosaur." The creature had large, flat plates all over its body.

Ankylosaurus's skull looks like it is divided into different sections. It looks almost like a stained glass window. The large, oval plates covering its body were called "osteoderms." These are small pieces of bone matter under the skin.

A second discovery a few years later helped scientists understand *Ankylosaurus* even more. Part of an *Ankylosaurus* tail was discovered in Canada in 1910. They saw that the tail had a huge knob at the end that looked like a club. They think *Ankylosaurus* probably swung its huge tail club to defend itself from attacks.

In 1947, the largest known *Ankylosaurus* skull was found in Canada. There have been very few other discoveries of *Ankylosaurus* bones. A full skeleton has never been found. Scientists aren't sure why *Ankylosaurus* **specimens** are so rare. One **theory** is that the dinosaur lived away from rivers and swamps. Areas with water are more likely to preserve fossils for many years.

Ankylosaurus was about twice the size of a rhinoceros.

Up close, *Ankylosaurus* probably had skin similar to a crocodile.

CHAPTER 2

What We Know

Ankylosaurus belonged to a group of dinosaurs that were all armored. The group is called ankylosaurs. The group is named after *Ankylosaurus* because it is the best-known dinosaur in the group. *Europelta* (yoor-oh-PELL-tah) was another ankylosaur. *Ankylosaurus* had a narrow beak that it used to pull leaves from plants. *Ankylosaurus* was one of the largest of the ankylosaurs.

When It Lived: 66 million years ago –
The Late Cretaceous Period
First Discovered: 1906, Montana

Ankylosaurus was a herbivore. This means it ate plants. It had a curved row of leaf-shaped teeth. Its teeth were helpful for cutting into plants that were low to the ground.

The short, wide, armored body of *Ankylosaurus* meant it could not run very fast. But it was too big and its skin was too thick for most other dinosaurs or animals to attack. It probably used its tail club in a few ways, including during **conflict**. Only a few fossils of its tail exist. But scientists have seen two examples of how the tail club could have been used. It may have needed to protect its territory against other *Ankylosauruses*. It may also have used its tail club to attract mates.

FUN FACTS

- *Ankylosaurus* had rows of spikes that ran along its body.
- The tail club of *Ankylosaurus* was likely strong enough to break the bones of another animal or dinosaur.
- *Ankylosaurus* means "fused" or "stiffened" lizard. This refers to its bony, armored structure.
- *Ankylosaurus* had a small brain that was about the size of two walnuts.
- *Ankylosaurus* is often compared to a military tank because of its armor. Some of its relatives even had armor on their eyelids.

THEN AND NOW

Ankylosaurus was one of the dinosaurs featured as a huge statue for the 1964–1965 World's Fair in New York. Visitors to Dinoland could see nine life-sized **fiberglass** dinosaurs. These included *Ankylosaurus*, *Triceratops* (try-SAYR-uh-tops), and *Tyrannosaurus rex*. In his extensive research on *Ankylosaurus*, **paleontologist** Kenneth Carpenter wrote, "The best-known ankylosaur in popular culture is *Ankylosaurus*, probably because it was featured as a life-sized reconstruction at the 1964 World's Fair in New York City."

Scientists believe *Ankylosaurus* could crush the bones of a *T. rex* with its tail.

Euoplocephalus and *Ankylosaurus* looked very similar to each other.

Ankylosaurus wasn't the only armored dinosaur. Here are a couple of others from the ancient world:

Hungarosaurus (hun–gah–roh–SORE–us): Most ankylosaurs lived in North America or Asia, but *Hungarosaurus* was from Europe. *Hungarosaurus* lived about 20 million years earlier than *Ankylosaurus*.

Euoplocephalus (yoo–ploh–SEF–uh–luss): *Euoplocephalus* lived earlier than *Ankylosaurus* but was very similar. It also had a tail club. Its bones are the most commonly found fossil of the ankylosaurs.

UP FOR DEBATE

Because so few *Ankylosaurus* fossils have been found, there is still a lot that paleontologists don't know about the dinosaur. Even some basics about *Ankylosaurus*, like its size, have been adjusted in recent years.

In 2004, paleontologist Kenneth Carpenter reexamined the small number of existing *Ankylosaurus* fossils. After doing that, he said that the maximum length of the dinosaur would've been 20.5 feet (6.2 m).

But a 2017 study used a method that relied on measuring the tail of *Ankylosaurus*. They used the tail length and compared it to other dinosaurs' tails. The 2017 study estimated that a large *Ankylosaurus* would almost certainly have been larger than the 2004 study concluded.

ANKYLOSAURUS
(ang-kuh-loh-SAWR-us)

Length: 23 feet (7 m)

Weight: 8,818 pounds (4,000 kilograms)

Top Speed: 6 miles (9.7 kilometers) per hour

Weakness: Very slow-moving

Best Weapon or Defense: Huge club at the end of its tail

EDMONTONIA
(ed-mon-TOH-nee-ah)

Length: 20 feet (6.25 m)

Weight: 6,000 pounds (2,722 kg)

Top Speed: 6 miles (9.7 km) per hour

Weakness: Very slow-moving

Best Weapon or Defense: Sharp spikes on its shoulders

CHAPTER 3

Keep Searching

Scientists are learning new things about dinosaurs every day. Developments in **technology** have helped scientists to build on each new discovery. They can also reexamine old fossils using new tools.

For a long time, scientists thought adult ankylosaurs lived mostly by themselves. Their armored bodies provided a natural defense. Once they were adults, it was thought that they did not need to travel in **herds** to protect themselves. But new research has presented a different opinion.

The research examined six different groups of ankylosaur bones found on three different continents. The ages of the dinosaurs in each group varied. This showed that in some cases, ankylosaurs did sometimes travel in herds. It isn't yet understood why that might have been. Maybe future discoveries will answer that question.

New dinosaur fossils are discovered around the world every day.

In 2020, scientists discovered a new member of the ankylosaur family. They called it *Sinankylosaurus* (sin–ang–kuh–loh–SAWR–uss), which means "Chinese fused lizard."

For as much as we know about the big, strong, armored dinosaur called *Ankylosaurus*, there is so much still to learn. Each new discovery of *Ankylosaurus* fossils and those of its relatives will help scientists paint a more complete picture of this dinosaur. Maybe YOU will make the next great *Ankylosaurus* discovery!

Scientists discovered a set of *Ankylosaurus* tracks in South America that are between 65 and 68 million years old.

GLOSSARY

armored (AR-murd): protected with a defensive covering

conflict (KON-flikt): a fight, battle, or struggle

fiberglass (FY-burr-glas): a material made from very fine threads of glass

fossil (FAH-sul): the remains or traces of plants and animals that lived long ago

herd (HURD): a large group of animals

K-T extinction event (K T ek-STINGKT-shun ee-VENT): the process, which included an asteroid impact, that led to the end of the dinosaurs 66 million years ago

paleontologist (pay-lee-on-TOL-uh-jist): a scientist who studies plants and animals that lived millions of years ago

prehistoric (pree-hiss-TORE-ick): belonging to a period in a time before written history

specimen (SPEH-seh-mehn): material used in testing, examination, or study

theory (THEER-ee): a group of linked ideas intended to explain something

WONDER MORE

Think About It: Scientists think *Ankylosaurus's* relative *Edmontonia* made a honking sound. Why do you think that is?

Talk About It: There are many different kinds of armor. Ask your friends or family to Imagine they were all dinosaurs. Would you rather have natural armor like *Ankylosaurus* or wear a metal suit of armor like a knight?

Write About It: Scientists are still discovering new kinds of dinosaurs. Imagine you could create a dinosaur to be a pet and live with you. What would it look like? How would it behave?

MESOZOIC ERA

Triassic Period	Jurassic Period	Cretaceous Period
201–252 Million Years Ago	145–201 Million Years Ago	66–145 Million Years Ago

LEARN MORE

BOOKS

Kelly, Erin Suzanne. *Dinosaurs*. New York: Children's Press, 2021.

Radley, Gail. *Ankylosaurus*. Mankato, MN: Black Rabbit Books, 2021.

Weakland, Mark. *Armored Dinosaurs: Ranking Their Speed, Strength, and Smarts*. Chicago: World Book, 2020.

WEBSITES

Visit our website for links about *Ankylosaurus*: **childsworld.com/links**

Note to Parents, Caregivers, Teachers, and Librarians: We routinely verify our web links to make sure they are safe and active sites. So encourage your readers to check them out!

INDEX

Asia, 15

Canada, 8
Carpenter, Kenneth, 13, 15
Cretaceous Period, 11

Euoplocephalus, 14–15
Europelta, 11

Montana, 7, 11

North America, 15

Sinankylosaurus, 20

Triceratops, 13
Tyrannosaurus rex, 4, 13

World's Fair, 13